salmonpoetry

Diverse Voices from Ireland and the World

the arts council
an chomhairle ealaíon

funding
literature
artscouncil.ie

NIGHTLIGHT
MARK WARD

Published in 2023 by
Salmon Poetry
Cliffs of Moher, County Clare, Ireland
Website: www.salmonpoetry.com
Email: info@salmonpoetry.com

ISBN 978-1-915022-28-8

Cover Image: *Inkspiral Design*
Cover Design & Typesetting: *Siobhán Hutson*

Printed in Ireland by Sprint Print

*Salmon Poetry gratefully acknowledges the support of
The Arts Council / An Chomhairle Ealaíon*

for Will

Contents

Bare

The only light comes from the distended
television – tinted with red, on heavy
rotation – lighting up limbs playfighting,
righting themselves into well-oiled hinges.

I watch your body reform, shivering
at cold spunk, aware of your breath's hardness
at my stare, you have become rudderless
in your quest to become nothing.

The world is a windowless tomorrow
holding steady on the brink of sunlight.
Fucked raw against the wall, there is a hush –
even your tinnitus is quiet now –

you're a skinflick burnt into the tv,
perpetually left precumming on mute.

Ten Steps to be Correctly Consumed by a City

for Eric Norris

dress like the person who
plays you in the movie
of your life; allow
marks on your skin (but worry
they're usurping); body parts
should become agents
of commotion; act like you're
artisan, hand-drawn;
stress like it's an artform;
bury the greenery of your accent
in collage; learn to think
inside the barrage of noise;
be aware every moment
each day is your choice;
your life, a gesture you
can't quite hold onto;
nor should you.

Cut-Up

I remember your face / You do?
Fingers fidget with hems
Cody / I'm Jack / Hours pass / I gotta see you again / You do?
Heartbeat errata, language failure

Face touch and hand plan
Your fingers are soft, mine are calloused /
Don't be so silly, they're fine
Shallow breath, in time to blinking

Associate stage hands write new lines
They pull the blinds as the over-the-clothes stuff
becomes more obvious, breathless, blind
The balcony wobbles in love

A Poem for Actors

after John Wieners

The room is filled with light
Our bodies heaving with air
We are present   in a way   no one
understands the lives we flee from

Documenting impermanence is a form of strength
This palmed love is codified among the slats where
we distil into performance   the lines alive
transformed in utterance from the author's burden

the audience's expectation   What this means
is our translucence   the utter destruction of days
For this is what we are made for   that
moment of disappearance where we are done

with pretending we are not the dawn
backlighting the empty stage   the applause   now
we are your disbelief   your pause at our encroaching night

The New World

San Francisco, 1945

I sit on the sidewalk and scuff
their uniform. Discharge papers crumple under my fist.
I watch the queer city swallow

the bus that brought me here,
the war. Each eyeful of this place claims its space in me.
The farm where I'm from: gone.

A familiar face, a nod, another.
Uniforms magnetise to each other. No parents, no pastor.
We are the tide, lapping the shore.

We room together for understanding.
We whisper about when they came, our names underlined,
unable to look us in the eye, or worse

the image of us at play spread across
their retinas. We disappeared with the magic of paperwork.
Our crimes coded in discharge colours,

we were supposed to go back to shame,
to static geography, work, family, to nice girls and monotony.
Instead, we chose the noise of this city.

We carve it around us, its buildings
sculpt our rhythms, our skin, our nights. Within each moment,
we are finally alive in the new world.

Gown

for Nell Regan

A reverse straight-jacket
not designed to close
no matter how hard I try
to tie the fabric strips –
I'm exposed. I pull on my
hoodie over hospital clothes.
I sit in the corridor.
My shins are cold.
I worry that someone could
see up what feels like a dress
that barely reaches my knees.
I have decorated myself for
cabaret, perfected Little Edie
Bouvier, lipsynched my way
through all the best parts,
a scattershot approach to drag
as art. I feel unsafe
as I wait for the ultrasound.
I watch myself pull down
the hem, zip up my hoodie,
cross my thighs so no one
can see – what? My bare legs?
My discomfort that for a moment,
I felt like a boy in a dress
and that, for a moment,
I allowed myself to feel less.

Exemplar

Nothing has been touched
for authenticity. The dirt,
their lives scattered across
this makeshift romance;
beds easily pushed apart,
bodies indent just like hearts
living for incognito weekends
away from friends, parents,
a life of false starts, pretence.

They notice only sanctuary,
a door shutting out the world
erasing borders, boundaries.
This is their chance, two boys
hushed with possibility, need,
bodies augment just like hearts
bleed into each other and mend
history. The boys pass through leaving
only the evidence of a memory.

Threads

Dad had me butcher the ends of my jeans –
the hems so frayed they could divine water

receding through neighbour's lips: a hiss, a tut,
a stare at its seams. My father imagines

the dirt of the day embedded inside
each thread; tangled slinkies, ripped tentacles

pulling on the jeans, the knees, their centre
of gravity, collapsing me in public.

Not me – I'm his son. His trousers starching
at the Medusa hairdo crowning my shoes;

each thread a sentient snake, complicit,
more eyes from which to prise forgiveness.

Turkish Bath

Under the railway arches,
a queer London imitation

with its own elliptical rituals;
a silent bartering for pre-residuals.

You're one of the contactables,
as Armistead once said.

*

Our groin and ass conjoining
the fiction that skin spins,

our rhythms supersede
the heavy gravity outside.

Each touch is a spotlight throwing
the rest of the world in darkness.

*

The steam is set-dressing
burying the cold sweat of your situation.

We chat about our impending
dissolution into stranger's lives.

You ladle water over stones
and disappear in their encroaching hiss.

*

I rinse. You shower thoroughly,
a surgeon blanching his skin.

A ghuzl, you correct me,
a ritual you couldn't possibly –

you towel off, leaving
me fouled, with no hot water.

Freddie

I remember
I was eight

alone in the living room

and the news
people said

you died.

I sobbed,
I didn't understand the word

'AIDS'

but I felt their eyes
through the screen

and I cried

like life
would kill me next.

Early Teenage Homosexuality

For Two or More Players

Rolling a one or two floods his hemisphere with bells,
alarm, an awareness of skin together; all this
causing an involuntary pulling apart. A stumble
down, out, and down the street. The heart
cannot take it. He withdraws into mute hatred.

A three or four and he goes through with it.
An affable desire to cum, not worried about
reassessing. It's just a thing. This result
lacks fear. There's some words of encouragement
as fingers climb. A smile. A kiss on the cheek.
Due to game mechanics, this roll is rare.

A five changes the game entirely.
You play to gain confident cocksucker cards,
and eventually the coming out card. Roll two dice
for twelve possible endings, ranging from good to bad
that don't really matter since there's no going back.

Roll a six, and you'll find someone like you
to go through all this with.

Dorsal

Adrift in a sea of cheap carpet,
the manes of the translucent horses
knit around a sail gathering wind.

Beneath the crosshatched fabric,
their bodies expand in the darkness;
their limbs act as icebergs, as sins.

Struggling for grip above quicksand,
their mouths mesh looking for purchase
as the mast flickers out, flickers in.

Breaths shared in time like a life vest,
they close their eyes in worship,
splitting the surface like a fin.

A Man in Love

for Ron Mohring

The wrinkles on my knuckles
split their seams coughing blood
in protest at your gutter mouth.

Your guttural protests seem
wrinkled from your spilt body,
knuckles dragging on the floor,

your coccyx bruising the dirt,
your body ragged and rankled
adrenalin flutters your hackles.

Sick cocksuckers, you raged,
holding your rankled ankle
wrinkled to you at right angles.

My fist flutters off your dirt,
my blood borders these gutters
that your cough tries to dispel.

Rebutted by this spell, your protest
is the itch in your throat unable
to wipe the love from his eyes.

Local

A knot of desiccated shopfronts
A festival comprised of four floats
A souvenir shop spills its unsold stock
        out onto the street

This town is a drive-thru
Its residents siphoned off into veins,
        bled into the outdoors
                space to oneself

The hill could be a mountain,
or a little up-and-over, a detour
of desire lines worn into earth;
the history of exploration, escape

plans. To meet the horizon,
one must become a cloud, a lance,
a microcosm, a vista, a picture
postcard to the folks without

trails laid out. The locals don't walk
here, they rescind their sky, allow
        meaning to disappear
behind daytripped days and eyes and

we imagine life in its confines, the splinter
between the pub and post office, home;
        a winter whose length you can walk
           without ever leaving

Blackbird

Cried out, I sit in the kitchen.
Mother busying herself within
its fridge and cupboards preparing
a wholesome farewell. She reviews her role
as parent, each conversation sifted through
for difference. She lays out the ingredients
on the counter in front of her.

She makes me a sandwich with her back to me
for a moment convincing herself
that I was her little boy again, about to go off
to school, excited about the world
but naïve enough not to be disappointed
by it. She wraps up the sandwich, all set,
and sags against the counter.

There's been a blackbird outside the window
for the past week. I knew something awful
was going to happen. She forgets that inside
I'm still that little boy that needs her always.
In practiced silence, she cries. I stare past her,
looking for birds and see only sky framing
our bodies; two ellipses, scattered into full stops.

The Office Carpet: A Mid-Afternoon Disaster Movie

I teeter on a corrugated sea
able to see down to its Mariana blue
seen when sat too close to the tv set.

The scuffmarks and stains are islands
as photographed from space. I sway
amidst them, each step vertiginous.

The cocksure office furniture
pretends not to float, imagines itself
as planets photobombing the picture

instead of a barbell held aloft
by a sea constricted by Christian tricks,
sick of the water being stolid.

The sea breathes; erupting, swallowing.
I cling to the doorframe and watch it all sink.

The Imaginary Friend

pinches inside the centre of my chest
like an axial graph folded and ripped,
an extradimensional shift to shit,
cinched with the rented smile of a guest

he suspects that his greatest achievement
is unravelling the probable
cause travelling without effect
leaving life only with the introspect

the what-ifs your standard issue rejects

he perfects his wind-tunnel soft whisper
appearing almost apologetic
at his fissures dotted around reality;
each idle thought an enemy, each slit

quickening the tangled nerves around it,
each brush becomes a thicket drowning
my vision and the waterline, revising
life into a supine circle of salt

Mongrel

This aroma is more than fleeting.
It's the stink of wet dog
washed with wire brush and soap;
punishment for uprooted flowers,
muddy paws, broken jars
and scratches on the door

that you left open, the door
that's always closed. Your shadow fleeting,
vanishes through the door ajar
like our hound did earlier, our dog
whom you wanted to call Flower
but I insisted we call Soap

'cause he'd never be clean, despite soap
and water, despite locking the door
until he learned not to eat the flowers,
until he learned that some pleasures are fleeting.
You bent down and stroked the dog
before giving him a treat from his jar

and the way you smiled at me jarred
as if you had decided to abandon your soap-
box for the barks of other dogs
that echo behind lines of closed doors
where debates are dead and scents are fleeting
apart from the stench of your shower gel; flowers,

no, something tart like citrus that drowns out the flowers
you brought into our kitchen and put in an empty jar,
a celebration of an anniversary, something fleeting
that sent you back to the shower and your soaps,
duty done. When dry, you head for the door
and resume your quest to become a dog

and today, your carelessness has confused our dog,
our obedient indoor pup doesn't know that flowers
are not for him, that he's an inside dog, that the door
is the limit of his world, that his treat jar
is used to keep him in line, that when I come armed with soap
it's about us, not him, but my tyranny is fleeting.

I nuzzle our dog, screw closed the jars,
throw out the half-eaten flowers, scour my hands with soap
and slump against the door, knowing that this isn't fleeting.

Circadian

I sleep. My body
alive at night
reading with the blue light
filter. Time to travel
through stories. I never sleep
enough. The morning
late enough for panic
I'm resigned to traffic.
Off-kilter, each step
teeters on total collapse.

I sleep through the totalled
morning. My body
resigned to filter time,
traffics panic enough at kilter
to sleep. I travel with light,
never reading for night's
collapse, each step
enough. The off-blue
teeters on. I'm alive.
Late.

Stopping Traffic

They treat it like a road;
the tarmac validated, flattened
with the beat of their feet.

A science-fiction set-piece:
the world forms underneath
as they walk on, oblivious.

It takes twenty decent steps
to cross. It's crass to wait
for approval. A stare-down.

Feral children pirouette
as a car materializes near.
Their screams a sheer stink.

Their hands a rabble, warning
the cars they're not compulsory.
A middle finger promissory note.

By the time the lights change,
the sidewalks are empty, frayed.
The drivers nervous, their eyes elope.

The signal to go. I check both ways.
The cars, done waiting, growl. The street
bows its head, so disappointed by me.

The Lads

the top deck almost imperceptibly
bristles at their back row bark
a child involuntarily looks past me
sees the taller one screaming
threatening that he would gladly go
to prison again that he would cut out
his throat and show him his voice
box the cunt his laughter a sonic boom
everyone staunch, stoic, staring at
their phones can they see mine
is now the time to watch *Drag Race*
his *again* the kicker until they see
will they turn their easy knife-like
rage onto me

I am thirty-five,
confident, and yet ready to make
allowances. I hit play defiant
but notice my left hand, its grip,
the angle obscuring. I can't concentrate,
I hear their music shrieking, their laughter,
a smell of shit. I don't turn around.
I have never hit anyone

                with intent
with a mobile phone screaming fury
he's back bellowing his conversation
an act of dominance what would we do
without this plugged-in civility
a contrite ignorance, our bodies
rely on rigidity and feigned casualness
the lads get up and saunter, pretending
not to watch how their weight displaces

our air, our breath, they're hawks
waiting to see a pair of eyes break
cover no one looks up it is over the top
deck a silent hymnal full of threats

Neurotic Break

Things go away.
Another paper-cut unpicks your skin

as if it were a Dear John, something
you carry around unopened

and thumb idly, knowing that
the seal is safe. Everything goes away

in the end. These tiny cuts wreck a life, take
the breath from your bones until you cannot

answer simple questions about
your current state.

Maybe I should
allow the wounds to stretch their legs

and get some air. I can feel the infection. I plan my
escape, each detail listed: fake names, a destination, what to do

in a new country. How to live with looking
over my shoulder. The creak will worsen as I get older.

Sink into inscrutable surroundings. Submit to the skit
of their sway.

Upon Seeing "A Streetcar Named Desire"

London, August 2014. For Collin Kelley.

I rest against the bar, the sobs subside. A headache
trumpets its arrival. With their applause,
the audience turned its face from the shadow;
Blanche DuBois, subsumed into their summer
night. Drenched from the day's rain, we came
as tourists, to be entertained by her destruction.

Fools think she does not see the world,
can only rose-tint it with fancy,
or, failing that, liquor. She can spot
the errant, the temporary through her haze,
can cast aspersions like prophecies
within which she is negated, free

to bounce to the best possible
circumstance, each reality tailored
to fit, each foundation born to cover
cracks. In her princess dress, Joker lipstick
smeared every body with blame. The heart
sometimes can no longer maintain.

Let us remember her disappeared face
as she is promenaded off, whilst guilt
roots everyone to the spot. She is calm
because there is no longer any history, or family,
or Blanche DuBois, just the sound of a body
slumping against strangers, hoping to stick.

I feel light-headed. I knock back two beers for the
shock, a learned behaviour from a southern belle.
Sometimes in life, people are not always saved
or punished. Sometimes you cry for the ending
you didn't get. You ask me if I'm okay, if I want
to go. The two-day rain has abated. Night is here.

Late Night at the Lethe

for Robert Pinsky

He sings –
a cuckoo exposed – of the outside:

the acknowledged girl, the suit and tie,
incongruous with this sort of recklessness,

hoping this admission will change him,
that the stinking river of shit beside him

will overpower everything, allowing life
to conspire the meeting between him

and me, searching for the means
to silence the crackle in our skins.

A lull in conversation, his fearful mouth fouls up
the sewer with the awkward cadence of decadence,

a drowning sung to an audience of echoes,
an edge of forcefulness to assuage the quiet

in which lives the soreness of untouched bodies,
ready to forfeit wives, careers, five-year plans.

He pants, staring. I have less to lose and steady
my bearings, my bare legs framed in the arch of another

turning, a deeper tunnel. Cars faintly fly overhead, unaware
of skin shedding, together unsullied, in guttural concert.

Valuation

We are all reduced
to numbers by numbers.
Figures. I must wait
for my superiors to die,
or Nomi Malone them down,
leaving behind their bank-seized
houses and below-market-value
salaries that I reach for
like a fought-for first breath
after a lungful of water.

We are all seduced
by dreams beyond our means.
Triggers. I deflate
as the interior allies
to blow down my home, drown
the naïve outline believed,
rouse and bellow my heartsick revue:
factories where life spawns
houses caught, coerced into blessed
laughter, a tongue like a solvent squatter.

Date

"Mr. you're on fire Mr. (No sir I'm okay)"
                                    – Liars

Canary Wharf. And feeling
like a speck among the glass everything:
corporate but pretentiously polite,
anaemia in real life.
I buy a new magazine
purely for its cover-mounted cd,
its unknown sounds displacing the waiting

among the shambling commuters.
This venue, a cut-through willed
into existence with dreams of dinner,
family, something returning, hurried.
No one is stuck waiting here
for IMs materialised into
midweek conversation, Italian food.

He was mid-to-late twenties,
shaved head – dinner in a restaurant, empty
even of us. He lived in a floating
apartment overlooking
the city. Stiff-necked talking,
neither of us remember walking
to the train station, unsure we're smiling;

grins, a pale imitation.
A missed connection. This isn't the city –
at least I tried. Leave it to its mystery.
I board the train to less than
this, to glances, elliptical cruising.
My Discman remembers where the song stopped.
It blares out mid-chorus, reasserting.

Trick

I laugh at boys that need to kiss
    to cum, that hit and miss
        brush of lips,

that slobbering mess subtle as a fisting
    your tongue as tender as kindling
        the moment dwindling

to a regret at not saving all of this
    for love, or for some lips
        that don't feel amiss

I curdle my mouth for those insisting
    on access despite being fleeting
        flesh designed for sweating

The rules explained about lips and nips
    about expectations, grips and flips
        about temporary eclipse

Our selfishness bartered tit for tit
    a transaction fulfilled bit by bit
        by bite, by spit, by grit

Until we give in to the seizure of bliss
    the mess of momentary happiness
        the mutual breathlessness

And when I can move, I start to dress
    aware that you seem to expect
        something more direct,

something you're not getting, my lips
mutter *goodbye, thanks, let's do this*
again, the same old script

trotted out once more for another trick
I head home, face flush, with a wish
for a boy whose lips I want to kiss

The Familiar

After being single for so many goddamn years, I realised that you were the most significant relationship in my life then. All we had in common were baser urges, we rarely spoke, and mostly a call came out of nowhere, after months of absence, asking if lips and skin could meet and smash against each other.

Early on, half of our stomping ground was a building site, empty shells of half-finished houses; the fourth wall missing for so long, it had been presumed non-existent. A perfect place to kneel and pray. The African security guard didn't know how to respond to me spitting you out, and casually saying hi, and days later was still confused as he grabbed me by the shoulders shouting, "Were you playing a game?" Smiling, I told him that of course I was and that I'd won.

Like a cruising cliché you wouldn't kiss, but at least you could, when pressed to, rationalise why. Cocks don't proclaim intimacy the way that tongues do. There's a submission in kissing that you can't just wish away. Apart from the odd time, when the lust level became too much, and you'd press me up against the posters on my wall, and kiss me like our heads could conjoin.

The years changed us; your hair is thinning, I moved away once, and have finally gone for good this time. Gone are your construction days and your deconstructed body, all hard chest and arms, and in its place, a paunch to match mine. Before I left, we sat on the edge of my bed, both in only boxer shorts, before beginning. I smiled happy, content that we were not the awkward teenagers we met as, full of furtive tugs, but that we were here, indoors, that we were men, together.

Mother Tongue

Chechnya, 2017

I say nothing. The police interrogate me,
start to break me with electricity. I scream but
say nothing. I will only live if I say nothing.
Each shock dissolves the words they speak,
the taunts they throw, they've always known,
my whole community responds with voltage.

I no longer understand their language.
I am a tourist mixed up in all of this
waiting for my embassy to free me
and be a near miss story I'll tell to the man
who loves me, who will never leave me
like this: eighteen, severed, unkissed.

I'm put in with thirty others; battery hens,
nowhere to move but for our sins, held
together by tears, the persistence of skin
and a confirmation, unintended by them,
that there are more of us. We cannot sleep so
we speak our secrets since it can't get any worse.

I jolt awake to see the boy beside me staring.
He's from a few villages over, yet we've never
met. The hand that woke me keeps contact, his lips
open slightly. I can't breathe looking at that. My first kiss
approaches. We're being watched. All I want is this
but I shake my head no; saying nothing, but living.

I lose track of days, of beatings. The wounds
no longer heal, keep bleeding. I am so thirsty,
I am starving. I cannot concentrate. I hear them
laughing. Or is that me when they ask me
questions. I will not speak. I will not lessen.
I'm dehydrated and delirious. I imagine a life

where I grow up somewhere else and this
would be a conversation, a status update,
an aspect of me. The village boy is dead.
I no longer sleep. I am a corollary. I dream.
There are millions like me, sleeping tonight.
I say nothing but still lose the fight.

Under, Neat

for Philip F. Clark

I bite at the socially acceptable
part of my body: the nail.
A tide held back by teeth,
the quick meets the skin,
the nerves threaten escape.

I pick my nails with themselves.
Occasionally the picker falters
becoming a sliver slid under
a nail, now all nerve,
a faltering, a chest tightening.

I press against it, feeling the flood,
a transmission underneath the skin.
Prodding, I control the traffic lights,
the reasoning. I catch my breath,
acclimatising, the lab rat failing the test.

Gristle

He gathers up your worries,
remnants or fully-formed
flurries, shorn of context.
He places them within a reflex,
reborn as certified causes
for his special effects, nerve ending
pyrotechnics, inhabiting each breath
that you can't quite catch.

With a lever pull, he's a pinball
breaking every light in the machine,
appropriating the bonus screen.
The flippers slick with sweat,
your fingers slip. You forget
the normalcy of your body at rest
becoming instead the conditional tense.

You wouldn't. You won't. You can't. You must.
Grist to the mill grinds you down to dust.

He plays your remains like a videogame.
Each Game Over erased with a Continue?
but you feel each death, each bullet, each sinew.
You're gristle, grasping at the NPCs
who respond to empty cues, a glitched script.
Help me, please. Their sunless smiles pixel burnt.
He debates whether he should quit or save.
Your dust reassembles, the game dissipates.

You're blinded by the outline of the day,
the shape of what it is without his sway.
Your body levels out. You forget this
affliction. For a moment; normality,
banality, an addiction to it;
the beauty of not noticing each breath.

Mobile Library

Mrs. P. loves to read poetry. Each month
I bring her an armful of books containing
a clash, a clattering of words, cascading
sounds stack like the skips of a scratched
poet trapped on a scraped cd. I carefully
clean its face and replace her old books
with new ones. I ask her if she has any
requests. She never does. She knows I'm a
poet. I dream of one day taking her my book.

Today, she was still in her stair lift,
her answering-the-door-wig in place
but she's flustered, panicked, aching.
Her eyes blurring, useless, her missing
spectacles no use, I help her into the chair
slowly. Everything hurts. Joints seize.
She feels the placement of her bones
like a flatpack skeleton taut, tightened,
braced for impact from any movement.

I navigate the unfamiliar kitchen,
make her a cup of tea, find the biscuits,
fill the pink furry hot water bottle,
the same colour as her leg blanket –
she can't tell the difference. I hunker
down beside her. She asks what she
should do now. I could call a doctor for
the pain or contact her family. *There
is nothing wrong enough for that*, she says,

What do I do now? I could get a neighbour?
Turn on the radio? She keeps telling me
to leave, that I'm busy. Her voice low,
apologetic at the burden. *God sent you*
to me today. I sit and hold her hand.
I want her to be okay. I want her to be
the bright bubbly lady I know. The brave face
is now mine to make but this is not about me.
I suggest diversions when she needs a solution.

She won't let me call anyone. *Someone will be*
here later. But she doesn't know who. I can't stay.
I don't want to leave. The weight of life in her face.
She tells me to visit if I'm around. Her books of poetry are
useless today. So am I. She thanks me again. I tell her
things will get better. She tells me that she just wants to die.
By-the-door goodbyes. *You're an angel.* The van door closes.
I cry like an orphan and pray for her wish to come true.

Jet Lag

not tiredness
                    a bodysnatched
sleep becomes
                    a terrorist
          surrounded
a continuous collapse
                    the bouncing ball follows
a wordless circle
                    of overlapped clock hands
the days now feign
                    a schedule except
they redirect
                    your body to run on
          empty
that nap erased
                    all sense of place
        incorrect
                    doors wilfully misplaced
this body could
                    be anyone's expanse
this room could
                    orbit back into place
        could redirect time's plans
my eyes askance

Basic Training

the sergeant does not like intentional rhyme
end of a line rhyme especially all that a-b-a-b
bullshit ballads the will-they-won't-they of
poetry he prefers the brutality of blank verse

its callous bark frees us from form and
technique the tool to embed multiplicity
rhyme is sophistry a fool needs to beautify
the world cannot be contained in stanzas

only a screamed refrain a sordid nickname
hissed like a cut throat can't hear the music
in his speech the put-on singsong of failure
repeats and this is where I start to write

Withdrawn

He is a cliff-
face looming
over the beach,
its sand an
afterthought
to its abrupt
landscape

He is a wall
of unscalable
chalk leaning
into its erosion:
unreturned calls,
hearing only wind,
I'll be gone soon

He longs to be
silt, unsentimental
when carried by
the roar of a river
to a sea where he's
sediment, an irrelevance
lining the ocean floor

Inheritance

the internal drone of being powerless
to protect your family as they traverse the day;
a fear of the permanence of words, opinions
braced like playing bumper cars with the street;
the ability to let a moment cast its light
despite the glare of life's undertow;
more empathy than you'll ever know
or want to know or think is fair;
the flair of telling a detailed story
diminished by overexcited repetition;
a calculated omission as punishment
whilst still adhering to work's guidelines;
one last visit to the bathroom before leaving,
wearing too many layers in this heat;
the spectacular feat of loving deeply
those who deserve you to;
a face and frame to grow into.

Diagnosis

Like the naming of a god; irrevocable,
the wrath of having the upper hand
temporarily, a name can plant seeds
scattering its shape across memories
until its laugh, soaked through with sweat,
derails the days utterly.

When you name a god, you must plan
your escape; impossible if they live inside,
if they hear your words before your face,
before your brain can fight them, can sieve
their on-high curses from your city.
Deities feel neither tiredness nor pity.

Naming a god is a marker, indelible,
a strikethrough linking distinct histories, episodes
unnamed, bad days, situations and mysteries
into the always capitalised A in Anxiety;
the lowercase days are erased entirely
leaving panicked flesh, shallow breaths, recovery.

You only name a god when you can
submit to the notion that you need saving.
You berate the body for the affront of drowning
in pinhole days, replays of relays of worst cases,
nursed traces of nuances in nuisances you patrol
the floodgates fixated by the weight of water.

Naming a god is a stark lore, irreversible,
each deviation from the carousel crippled
with diagnosis, you wonder if this is it
again, each day framed with a battlement,
where repeated refrains let your nerves relent,
and lapse into silence, for a moment, content.

The Doctors Say

I mustn't use my body as a dance move,
as a way for me to prove the voices
wrong; that we are rash choices,
that without the coupling we're just skin.
You can't deny the smile that comes
with cumming, there's a silent thrum
shared, *he loves me*, but I knew this.
I'm just scared that without proof it's
beyond my reach, something I can lose.

I cannot use my body as I choose,
as a way to just shut up and play the hits;
songs we make up with our jigsawed bliss,
a shared light widening until we're thin,
unthinking, breathless, cramping, voiceless.
Today they say that I must change the noises,
the method. My body is a bleeding gum.
I feel your fearless tongue, our bodies' scrum,
your viscous grin I could never disprove.

Public Displays of Affection

for Saul Ward

Today, kissing is a competition.
A sloppy act of composition.
A brush of lips as intermission,
as political tract.

I watch them instinctively act
upon their biological fact.
Their sexuality as ruling pact,
as walking exposition.

Hand-in-hand, each story's transcription
into shared history occurs by validation;
eyes fix upon their smug radiation.
They glance to their audience, rapt.

Each performance whispers of subscription
since monopolies stay so with repetition.
Each grazing tongue staves off depletion,
is another way to distract

from those unwilling to follow instruction
and uncover the mysteries of opposition;
two different bodies designed for collision,
for maximum impact.

Their bodies like an action movie in abstract;
reduced to insertion, condensed to contract,
abbreviated out of context as a pornographic act
like the way they see my life; as an act of attrition

decaying my willpower by building partitions,
saying what I can do, what's up for discussion,
what's acceptable in public, what causes revulsion
and how to live when life subtracts.

The man and woman stop and kiss. I overreact.
They're holding up the queue, I turn away and redact
their kiss. Their happy bliss. Life moves on intact
but I feel like my mouth is close to sedition,

however, you don't like public displays of affection
You smile softly at my silent act of volition
to write this poem and end it with us, eyes-closed, kissing
as protest, as an expression of love, as something matter-of-fact.

Apologia

I breathe inside your body like a lung.
You are aware I'm also breathing out.
You close your eyes and try to bite our tongue.
You needn't worry – I can always shout
across your silences, attempts at peace,
I amplify the chatter into noise.
You start to ground yourself to make me cease
but I possess the darkness in your voice.
I flood your brain and body with fresh guilt,
a stimulus, response, it must be true;
through tears you realise I am what you built
and I exist only because of you.

Shark Tank

Muted, I vibrated out of my skin
'til it sweat out an EMP, smashing
the hallway's glass aquariums, flooding
the doors open, then, my presentation
begins. I believe in my business but
my metaphor is sodden with crying
and we have dead air with millions watching
the evaluations and the doors shut.
Intrusive close-ups, no one wants to go
out. Even now with so much uncertain
your arms around mine are all that I know,
all that I was is now undetermined.
My words have undone our world, now we wait

Recognising Similes

He speaks like I was unable to.
By the time my words came through,
they were a torrent; I was crying like
a burst dam had breached my body
leaving only erosion, water damage.

I overhear his testimony, words lancet
through skin; *overworked, exhausted,*
the twitch is stress, mindfulness.
I recognise the boy I used
to be. I dither at the similarity.

I went through it too. No time
to be sick. Too busy to fall
apart. Fall apart. Claim the sofa.
Rest your head, your heart. Let yourself
be sick. Speak. Get better, get through it.

He asks me if I did, if I am, whether
the tablets, the talking, all went to plan.
They did. He doesn't need to know
my life is now a histogram, that I am
forever aware what it feels like to unravel.

An Avalanche, Interrupted

after Thom Gunn

Fear is too filling a meal for a feast.
More wine taste than blood test, you sip, you spit.
You swallow the security you've leased.
Your body a shield, ready to remit.

Each pill a prayer, a deathless canary.
Its vigilant glare precludes the prairie.

The man with the night sweats isn't alone.
Their physiques perspiring with skin on skin
Heat only another body can bring.
On loan to himself, he feels truly known.

Each pill is practice, an affirmation
Waiting for tomorrow, now impatient.

Vegas Epithalamion

for Will

A shirt of fireworks, a burst
of colour off in the distance,

falling slowly to an ombre.
A plain black shirt adorned with names,

two men's names; Harley, Davidson;
the mundane queerness of arms

wrapped around, riding pillion.
Two black bands are offset against

pale Irish skin reacting to
mandatory cigarette smoke

usurping the air entirely.
Down a side street, we breathe easy

in the tiny glass chapel
with its too-thin aisle designed

to have and to hold each other.
The celebrant's script is laminated

so we do not expect it to resonate
and make us cry the way it does.

Here is love, facing each other.
We say it's not legal, and it isn't –

the paperwork and party yet to come –
but as the minister goes off script

with an ad lib, correctly guessing his audience,
you follow this with your vows, unrehearsed

and flawless. I couldn't love you more than this.
My words stumble at the grace yours had

and I speak plainly, but inarticulate,
sideswiped by the beauty of the moment,

so this is how I make up for it.

Acknowledgements & Notes

Some of these poems, often in earlier versions, appeared in the following journals:

Animal	'Dorsal'
Assaracus	'Cut-Up', 'Early Teenage Homosexuality', 'The Familiar' and 'Turkish Bath' (as 'Turkish Delight')
Banshee	'Threads'
Bleached Butterfly	'Neurotic Break'
Boyne Berries	'Public Displays of Affection'
Cordite	'Apologia' and 'The Doctors Say'
Emerge	'Mongrel'
The Failure Baler	'Stopping Traffic' and 'Valuation'
Glitterwolf	'Upon Seeing "A Streetcar Named Desire"'
The Good Men Project	'Basic Training'
HeadStuff	'Ten Steps to be Correctly Consumed by a City' and 'The Imaginary Friend'
HIV Here + Now	'Bare', 'Freddie', 'Gown' and 'Under, Neat'
Icarus	'Inheritance', 'Diagnosis' and 'A Man in Love'
The Irish Times	'Mobile Library'
The New Verse News	'Mother Tongue
Off the Rocks	'The New World'
Softblow	'Gristle', 'Jet Lag' and 'The Office Carpet: A Mid-Afternoon Disaster Movie'
Studies in Arts and Humanities	'Blackbird'
Tincture	'Local'
Vast Sky	'Exemplar'
Visual Verse	'Circadian'
Wussy	'Date', 'The Lads' and 'Late Night at the Lethe'

'An Avalanche, Interrupted' and 'A Poem for Actors' first appeared in *Lovejets: Queer Male Poets on 200 Years of Walt Whitman*, edited by Raymond Luczak.

'Vegas Epithalamion' was first broadcast on RTÉ Radio 1 show *Arena* on 20th June 2019. It subsequently appeared won 2nd place in the 2019 Bray Literary Festival Poetry Competition, and appeared in print in *Public Displays of Affection: Poetry Ireland Introductions 2020*, alongside 'Public Displays of Affection' which was reprinted there.

'Withdrawn' was first broadcast on The Poetry File on Evelyn Grant's Weekend Drive on RTÉ Lyric FM on 18th July 2020. It was first published in *Queering the Green: Post-2000 Queer Irish Poetry*, edited by Paul Maddern.

'A Poem for Actors' is a terminal from the second section of John Wieners' poem, 'Acts of Youth', and is partly inspired by his 'A poem for painters'.

'Dorsal' was inspired by Robert Dash's collage, 'Into the Mystic'. (www.robertdashphotography.com)

Thanks

– to the editors who first published these poems: Stuart Barnes, Ariana D. Den Bleyker, Michael McKeown Bondhus, Bryan Borland, Matthew Bright, Michael Broder, Angela T. Carr, Ciaran Carty, Laura Cassidy, Patrick Chapman, Nathan Currow, Kate Dowling, Allison Fradkin, Nicholas Goodly, Punk Groves, Claire Hennessy, Eric Low, Raymond Luczak, Paul Maddern, Sam Murphy, Stephen S. Mills, Lori A. Minor, James Penha, Eimear Ryan, Preti Taneja, Sophie Furlong Tighe, Cyril Wong and Daniel Young.

– to Jessie Lendennie and Siobhán Hutson for making my lifelong dream come true.

– to the OGs: Aimee MacLeod, Ciara Pelly, Anne Sexton, Dermod Moore, Richard Ryan, Ciaran Scolard and Kiara Gannon.

– to all the readers of my chapbook, *Circumference*, and special thanks to its loudest supporters: Paul Burston, Jerry L. Wheeler, Jeff Mann, Deirdre Sullivan, 'Nathan Burgoine, and Andrew Howdle.

– to Ron Mohring for believing in *Carcass*, to Katy Naylor for encouraging me to play around with *Faultlines*, and to Stuart Buck for allowing me to go on a *HIKE* in Bear Creek.

– to Words Ireland who awarded me a mentorship under the 2018/2019 National Mentorship Scheme, and to Nell Regan, whom I worked with closely on these poems, and who transformed my writing.

– to those who read early drafts of this book: Raymond Luczak, Philip F. Clark and Ron Mohring (again!), with an extra-special thanks to Collin Kelley.

– to all of my family, but in particular to my father Richard, my sisters Karen, Richelle and Shonagh, and my nephew Saul: you have all been so encouraging in my dream to be a poet, and cannot be thanked enough.

– to Eric Norris, the most patient, kind, intelligent critic, poetical midwife and friend a boy could ask for: *il miglior fabbro*.

– to William McLoughlin, everywhere I look in this book you are there and this book would not be here without you. Thank you for everything.

MARK WARD is the author of the chapbooks *Circumference* (Finishing Line Press, 2018), *Carcass* (Seven Kitchens Press, 2020), *Faultlines* (Voidspace, 2022) and *HIKE* (Bear Creek Press, 2022). As well as appearing in many journals, both at home and abroad, he has featured in numerous anthologies, including the landmark *Queering the Green: Post-2000 Queer Irish Poetry* (The Lifeboat Press, 2021). He was Highly Commended in the 2019 and 2022 Patrick Kavanagh Awards and in 2020 was selected for Poetry Ireland's Introductions Series. In 2021 and 2022, he was awarded bursaries from the Arts Council of Ireland. He is the founding editor of *Impossible Archetype*, a biannual international journal of LGBTQ+ poetry.

salmonpoetry

Cliffs of Moher, County Clare, Ireland

"Publishing the finest Irish and international literature."
Michael D. Higgins, President of Ireland